Big Cat phonic readers:
The Sun and the Moon

In Big Cat phonic readers the specific phonemes and tricky words being focussed on are highlighted here in these notes, so that you can be clear about what your child's learning and what they need to practise.

While reading at home together, there are all sorts of fun additional games you can play to help your child practise those phonemes and tricky words, which can be a nice way to familiarise yourselves with them before reading, or remind you of them after you've finished. In *The Sun and the Moon*, for example:

- the focus phonemes are igh (night), y (sky), ay (away), a-e (pale), i-e (shine), y (very/rocky). Why not write them down and encourage your child to practise saying the sounds as you point to them in a random order. This is called 'Speed Sounds' and as you get faster and faster with your pointing, it encourages your child to say them as quickly as possible. You can try reversing the roles, so that you have a practice too!

- the tricky words are 'the', 'to', 'all', 'you', 'do', 'some', 'because', 'there', 'no', 'come' and 'they'. You can play 'Hide and Seek' by asking your child to close their eyes and count to 10, while you write each word on a piece of paper, hiding them somewhere in the room you're in or the garden for your child to find. As they find each one, they should try reading and spelling the word out.

Reading together

- Why not start by looking at the front cover of *The Sun and Moon* and talking about what you can see.

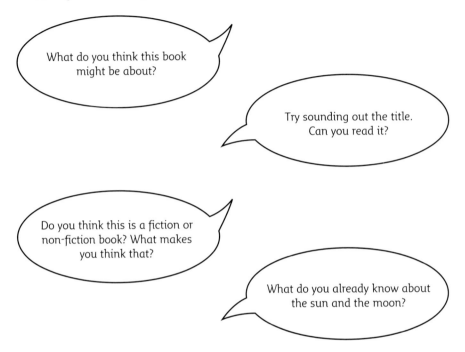

What do you think this book might be about?

Try sounding out the title. Can you read it?

Do you think this is a fiction or non-fiction book? What makes you think that?

What do you already know about the sun and the moon?

- Enjoy reading *The Sun and the Moon* together, noticing the focus phonemes (igh, y, ay, a-e, i-e, y) and tricky words (the, to, all, you, do, some, because, there, no, come, they). It's useful to point to each word as your child reads, and encouraging to give them lots of praise as they go.

- If your child gets stuck on a word, and it's phonetically decodable, encourage them to sound it out. You can practise blending by saying the sounds aloud a few times, getting quicker and quicker. If they still can't read it, tell them the word and move on.

Talking about the book

- Talk about the facts about the sun and moon on pp18–19, what additional facts can you add to this?

- Practise the focus phonemes from *The Sun and the Moon* by asking your child, for example, what sound 'away' ends with, and how to sound out, for example, 'night'.

The Sun and the Moon

Written by Paul Shipton

Collins

You can see the sun shine in the daytime.

Do not look right at the sun. It is bad for you.

You can see the moon shine
at night.

On some nights the
moon looks yellow.

On some days you cannot see the sun because of clouds, but the sun is still in the sky.

On some nights you can just see part of the moon.

On some nights you can see all of it.

The moon is round.

The sun seems to travel across the sky. At lunchtime, it is high in the sky. In fact, our planet spins around. This makes the sun seem to travel across the sky.

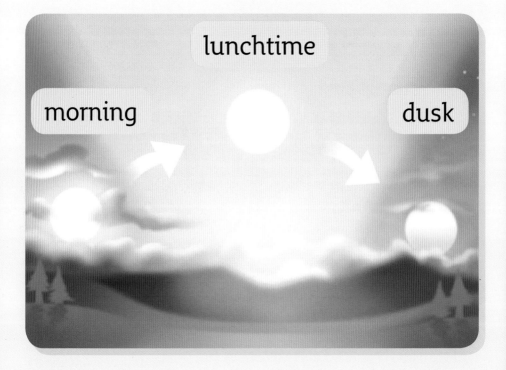

morning

lunchtime

dusk

You see the moon in different parts of the sky at night. This is because the moon travels around our planet.

The sun is very big. It is made of very, very hot gas. The sun is a star.

Our planet travels around the sun.

The moon is not as big as our planet. The land is very rocky. There are no animals or plants.

All of our light and heat comes from the sun. The sun is much too hot to visit.

Some men did visit the moon in a rocket. They stuck a flag up there.

This man is standing on the moon.

You can jump very high on the moon. You can throw things a long way.

On some days you can see
the moon in the daytime, too.
It looks very pale in the sky.

You cannot see the sun at night, but you can see lots of different stars. They do not look the same as the sun because they are far, far away.

The Sun

- You can see the sun in the daytime.
- The sun is round.
- It is made of very hot gas.

The Moon

- You can see the moon at night.
- The moon is round.
- It is very rocky.

Getting creative

- Have some fun with your child by playing a running game, where they run, hop or jump towards different focus phonemes written on pieces of paper and stuck around the room. For example they could run to the 'igh' phoneme, hop to the 'ay' phoneme or jump to the sound at the end of 'rocky'.

- To practise the tricky words, why not play 'Fast Words', where you write all the tricky words down on a piece of paper and point to each one for your child to read, getting faster and faster!

- If your child's interested in this book, spend some time talking about the diagram on p10 and about how the earth spins and how the sun and earth move.

- Together think up some good words to describe the sun and moon, and encourage your child to have a go at writing them down.

Other books at Level 2:

Fiction	Non-fiction
The Singing Beetle — Linda Strachan, Oliver Hurst	The Rainforest at Night — Nic Bishop
Zog and Zebra — Mal Peet and Elspeth Graham, Sarah Horne	Gorillas — Teresa Heapy
A Day Out — Petr Horáček	The Sun and the Moon — Paul Shipton

Collins Big Cat
Reading Lions

Published by Collins
An imprint of HarperCollins*Publishers*
1 London Bridge Street
London
SE1 9GF

© HarperCollins*Publishers* 2006
This edition was published in 2015.

Author: Paul Shipton

Paul Shipton asserts his moral right to be identified as the author of this work.

British Library Cataloguing in Publication Data
A catalogue record for this publication is available from the British Library.

Illustrator: Blair Sayer
Designer: Niki Whitehorn, niki@whitehorndesign.co.nz
Parent notes authors: Sue Reed and Liz Webster

Acknowledgements
Front cover: Science Photo Library; Back cover, p1r, p5b, p9, p11, p15: NASA; p1l, p8, p14: SOHO (ESA & NASA); p2: Alamy/Aqua Image; p3: Science Photo Library/Martin Dohrn; p4, p5: Frank Lane Picture Agency/Minden Pictures/Jim Brandenburg; p10: Photolibrary.com (Australia); p12: Alamy/Photo Network; p13: Science Photo Library/ Frank Zullo.

Printed and bound by RR Donnelley APS

www.collins.co.uk/parents